# Dark Ink
# And
# Whispers.

## Samantha Ann

ISBN:
978-0-578-41723-3

# CONTENTS:

# DEDICATION:

### Jennifer Peters (Mrs. Tavares)
For recognizing my talent before anyone else and supporting me the entire way.

### Ruthann & Janice
May the books in heaven be as beautiful as you both. Thanks for always being there, even when you're gone.

### Christopher
For loving me always, through thick and thin.

# Somber for Desire

Far from empty,
absorb the light,
flashing by like a train at night,
the quicker we go,
the more we stumble,
Listen as the night starts to rumble.
Dipped in desire
and soaked in somber,
Learn to endure all thats stronger.

# Alive

My thoughts, they hurt.
Like ember,
They burn until only ash is left.
Corroded and full of smoke,
Where are the mirrors?
My bliss is only content,
if my thoughts cry,
I must form a storm that cannot die,
Just to keep my fire alive.

# Writer's Mind

Writer's are mad in the most sane way,
their minds twist and curve
into the darkest place,
The slightest light keeps them full.
A light that turns death,
that turns skies,
that turns souls,
into a garden full of bloom,
a garden that was once nothing,
But death and doom.

# Night and Day

When the earth closes it's eye's,
everything else does the same,
the warm sheets suddenly feel cold,
the blissful songs outside turn quiet,
and the smooth thoughts in your mind,
Become rapid.
As if your brain were a reflection,
of night and day,
bat your lashes,
and take a glimpse,
Just timidly sweep away.

# Burn Away

We are taught to survive,
but not how to live,
stance on the world for all it gives,
we are not unbloomed,
like the meadow of death,
we are born to blossom,
through the slightest of breath,
as of winter,
crisp and cold,
grasp onto the stars,
As if they were our own.
Prosper the day,
achieve the night,
we are simply candles,
blazing away the surrounding light,
So burn, burn, burn away.

# Melancholy Rays

He looked into my eye's,
to a place no other has seen,
he asked me,
are you a happy
Or sad person?
I suppose,
I'm a little bit of both,
Like the moon on a sunny day.

# Black and Lilac

Like an old film,
the moment was silent,
dull like black and white,
she laid upon her lilac sheets,
with thoughts in her eye's,
a tornado was progressing inside her soul,
and it wouldn't be much longer,
until all poison became dust.
She was happy,
finally,
A bliss that couldn't be taken.

# Lingering Lust

If I died today,
Would you love me tomorrow?
if I cried tonight,
Would you hug me in my sorrow?
if we were all that's left,
Would I still be the one?
the one who lingers,
like a rose in the sun,
reaching for my thorns,
just to be touched,
together,
We form unbearable lust.

# Singed

My mind is a twisted tree,
in which the branches consume me,
it fills me with holes,
gaps of torn soul,
like a garden thats singed,
I am heavy with fringe,
but yet,
I still manage to stand,
I'm a page ripped from a book,
That still feel hands.

# Woe

I asked for a rose,
but not the flower,
a color so delicate,
it lives yet dies every hour,
like hope hovers,
on lover's lip's,
it's the little white lie,
we attach at the hip,
keep it safe,
don't let it go,
our sanity craves it,
Like a heart to its woe.

# Soul Full

The freckles on my nose are stars,
forming constellations upon my bones,
above,
my eye's are an autumn moon,
Leaving senna cast upon like stones.
inside I can feel growth,
a garden of rose at bloom,
and the potential yearning beneath my porcelain skin,
as it cracks it begins to thin,
and reveal my inner slate,
like ink on a page,
I bleed and run,
in hopes to discover,
a never ending world.
somewhere beneath these senna eye's,
There is someone so full of life.

# Watercolor Waves

Shades of orange and red flicker,
in the distance,
like a candle at it's peak,
the sky grows dim,
as the mist sets in,
But I can't dare look away.
when I stare at the ocean,
I feel a sense of rush
and in that moment
I feel life's thoughts,
As if I were the key to every locked door.
I want to feel that way everyday,
If only I were the waves crashing down,
like the lashes on my eye's,
then the thoughts in my brain would melt,
like a watercolor sunset,
I'd be free.

# Silent Love

Silence is a metaphor,
that only we can follow,
nearby the rain is falling,
but we remain still,
our bodies,
warm,
wrapped in each other's skin,
intertwined,
like vines on a brick house,
a love that envelopes,
a desire to feel
the weather outside can't compare,
the storm in our eye's,
It's stronger than most.

# To Feel

To feel is to hurt
an abundance of red,
touching without a notice,
like a flower,
who can't see its bloom,
seeing with eye's,
that are filled of question,
don't doubt the belief of realism,
just breath,
so deep you can almost drown,
to feel is to hurt,
Even if there is no one around.

# Old Soul

I have an old soul,
the kind that gathers dust,
sitting like gold,
on a shelf among brass,
fulfilled in stained glass,
I encase myself in the pages,
like the ink to a quill.
breathing in all the particles.
that form decades of life,
each worth living through,
Immortality at its' best.

# A Pretend Reality

There's a conundrum in my brain,
it feeds on envy and horrid things,
puzzled and lost,
reality is gone,
may it be sweeter to dream,
than to live in a world without love,
without virtue,
without sensation for spirit,
may we all just dream,
that reality is more than our dreams can reach,
settled into a haven of painless hurt,
and fearless scare,
Dream until there is no more pretending.

# Autumn Nights

The night was cold and crisp,
like autumn's fall,
soaking the mist into my pores,
like a dry sponge,
I watched as the Sienna leaves danced away,
carrying my heart with every sway,
I can hear the longing in my soul,
it screams for purpose,
for desire,
for any and all,
but on this autumn night,
I have no thoughts,
I'm simply as the moon,
Just quietly waiting to disappear.

# Summertime Holly

When two souls meet,
they almost whisper,
Like the way clouds kiss before a twister.
Passion or lust?
love is both
Dipped in heaven and destine for growth.
love appears like a mist at bay,
Never when you see light of day.
he's wrapped in summer,
and her in holly,
But their fire burns hotter than Bali.

# Envy

Envy is green,
like the color of her eye's,
she trembles and folds,
to hold herself at ease,
but envy is green,
and she's lying in grass,
if the season were spring,
she would be hollow,
fighting just to stay,
stay above all that's green,
And deeply trapped in between.

# Saintful Sinners

The world is filled with sinner's,
and those of saintliness hand's,
like a bee in a wasps nest,
Where can we stand?
fallacious lip's,
brim with echos of doom,
saintful sinner's are malignant,
like a dark tomb,
the line between us,
is as fine as day,
How can we stand, when all is just gray?

# Darlings

Dangling from ourselves
like a spider stuck in it's web,
our hand's gripping the shelves,
even though you're lying in bed,
you must kill your darling's to feel alive,
you must kill your darling's just to survive,
the trees' nearby giggle with grief,
standing among those with belief,
to kill your darling's,
is to kill the dark,
Just let your fear disembark.

# Wake

Wake up,
you are not asleep,
drenched in melancholy,
and dripping with defeat,
wake,
to see the sun rise,
wake,
to kiss the moon goodnight,
wake,
to feel the beating of my heart,
envelope every beat,
just wake up,
to assimilate all the world,
And be so ever close to me.

# Sometimes

When you love something,
it becomes your's,
a tiny piece of a forever bond,
even if the love leaves,
a piece of it will never go,
like a scar that continues to rise,
wounds may heal,
but real pain burns,
sometimes love,
leaves scars that may not hurt,
Sometimes love is all our sadness needs.

# Cold

Like a cold blanket,
cloaking my limbs,
my soul is filling with snow,
So pure it hurts,
ember melting away,
burning like dry ice,
the cold inside me is numb,
crumbling as winter does,
let the ember melt it away,
let the coldness have it's day,
Let the blue turn bright again.

# Murmurs

Theres talk and whispers among the walls,
like smoke from a pipe,
or lips from a note,
unseen and hallow but full of rage,
Do you see the angels standing among the stage?
they cry with empathy for those without breath,
the crimson curtains are falling to their death,
wonderland is a real place,
for those with broken hearts
And those without grace.

# Grandma

Silence gathered the room as part of her left us,
the beeping from her heart was longer alive,
like the butterflies that use to dance in her garden,
and the blue in her eye's it has drifted somewhere unknown,
Almost as if she were lost as sea.
She was gone.
she was silent like thought's in our brain,
Her's was no longer there.
It's all just a blur, a blur of color and numbness.
Silence is the moment when everything around you changes.
As you kiss someone goodnight the silence of that moment
is infinite.
Part of you if being giving to that person.
The silence from the dreams in your mind carry you through
part of this world no one else has seen.
silence takes part of something that once was here and gives
it to something new,
something we no longer see
But know that wherever it is it's meant to be.
the petals began to fall
and the leaves began to shed from what once was something
so full,
she was a rose,
That's now wilted and yet so beautiful.

# Fearful flowers

We are all just flowers in a garden somewhere,
waiting to be picked or smashed,
but sometimes,
it's the mystery that keeps our garden alive,
like the smell of rain when you don't know it's near,
we are all just trembling with fear,
fear that allows stems to grow and petals to bloom,
Sometimes fear is what heals us the most.

# Snowflake Stars

Everlasting stars glisten in the night,
like a snowflake that doesn't melt,
I hear the moaning from the moon,
as the howls of night fill my room,
my shadow is dark against the glow,
much like my mind,
it's brimming with woe,
the smokey clouds cover my skin,
I am among the stars,
A star full of snow,
Full of hope.

# Life After Death

Life and death are much the same,
black, white and full of dawn
like a window with no lock,
who's to say where the line ends?
who's to say where one may begin?
for those who grieve,
you are much alive,
for those who breathe,
you are much asleep,
but who's to say we cannot be rife?
may a garden grow from my pale soul,
The same as a garden may grow in the sun.

# Insane Sanity

She became insane,
from hoarding sanity too long,
she was much like a bird,
who finally learned to see in the dark,
to be sane is more severe,
than to be mad in all forms,
ludicrous,
bizarre,
the odd one's live on,
because there is no light,
Without some form of peculiar darkness.

# Dream of Dreaming.

I often dream of dreaming,
a piano with no tune,
I play the notes as if they will sing,
but disappointment cloaks the room,
the glass walls reflect,
and I stare back hard,
I'm simply the string of a dusty harp,
dreaming to be tuned,
I often dream of dreaming,
a realm with no purpose,
but I often feel the key's,
Just to be the illusion.

# Sunflower

"I'm not okay" She thought,
withholding the truth,
like a damm full of sadness,
she was about to break,
crumbling bricks that shatter like glass,
her insides were mangled in a web,
a web that couldn't dissolve,
she was trapped,
and just waiting to wilt,
she was a sunflower
without a sun
But still managed to grow so strong.